SPOTLIGHT ON GEORGIA

GEORGIA DURING THE AMERICAN REVOLUTIONARY ERA

SAM CROMPTON

PowerKiDS press.

NEW YORK

Published in 2018 by The Rosen Publishing Group, Inc.
29 East 21st Street, New York, NY 10010

Editor: Theresa Morlock
Book Design: Rachel Rising

Photo Credits: Cover, p. 21 North Wind Picture Archive; p. 4 https://commons.wikimedia.org/wiki/File:French_and_indian_war_map.svg; p. 5 MPI/Stringer/Getty; p.7 Courtesy of the Library of Congress; p. 9 https://commons.wikimedia.org/wiki/File:SavannahColony.JPG; p. 11 Hargrett Rare Book and Manuscript Library, University of Georgia Libraries; p. 13 Watkins, Robert and George Watkins. A Digest of the Laws of the State of Georgia. Philadelphia: Printed by R. Aitkin, No. 22, Market Street, 1800; p. 13 (background) Reinhold Leitner/Shutterstock.com; p. 15 Courtesy of The New York Public Library Digital Collections; p. 17 https://commons.wikimedia.org/wiki/File:Soldiers_in_Uniform_WDL2960.png#/media/File:Soldiers_in_Uniform_WDL2960.png; p. 19 https://en.wikipedia.org/wiki/Battle_of_Kettle_Creek#/media/File:Kettle_Creek_Battlefield_~_Wilkes_County,_GA.JPG; p. 23 Georgios Kollidas/Shutterstock.com; p. 24 Hulton Archive/Stringer/Getty Images; p. 25 Historical Picture Archive/Contributor/Getty Images; p. 27 Fotosearch/Stringer/Getty Images; p. 29 https://commons.wikimedia.org/wiki/File:Surrender_of_Lord_Cornwallis.jpg

Cataloging-in-Publication Data
Names: Crompton, Sam.
Title: Georgia during the American Revolutionary era / Sam Crompton.
Description: New York : PowerKids Press, 2018. | Series: Spotlight on Georgia | Includes index.
Identifiers: ISBN 9781508159711 (pbk.) | ISBN 9781508159742 (library bound) | ISBN 9781508159728 (6 pack)
Subjects: LCSH: Georgia--History--Revolution, 1775-1783--Juvenile literature. | Georgia--History--Juvenile literature.
Classification: LCC F289.C76 2018 | DDC 975.8'02--dc23

Manufactured in the United States of America

CPSIA Compliance Information: Batch #BS17PK For further information contact Rosen Publishing, New York, New York at 1-800-237-9932.

CONTENTS

CHAPTER ONE

LEADING UP TO WAR

The American **Revolution** was the outcome of years of growing conflict between the 13 colonies and Britain. After the Seven Years' War, Britain was deeply in **debt**. In 1763, King George III issued a proclamation making it illegal for colonists to move across the Appalachian Mountains. Starting with the

The Seven Years' War was a clash between France and Britain over **imperial** territories. The French and Indian War was the part of the Seven Years' War fought in North America. The war lasted from 1756 to 1763.

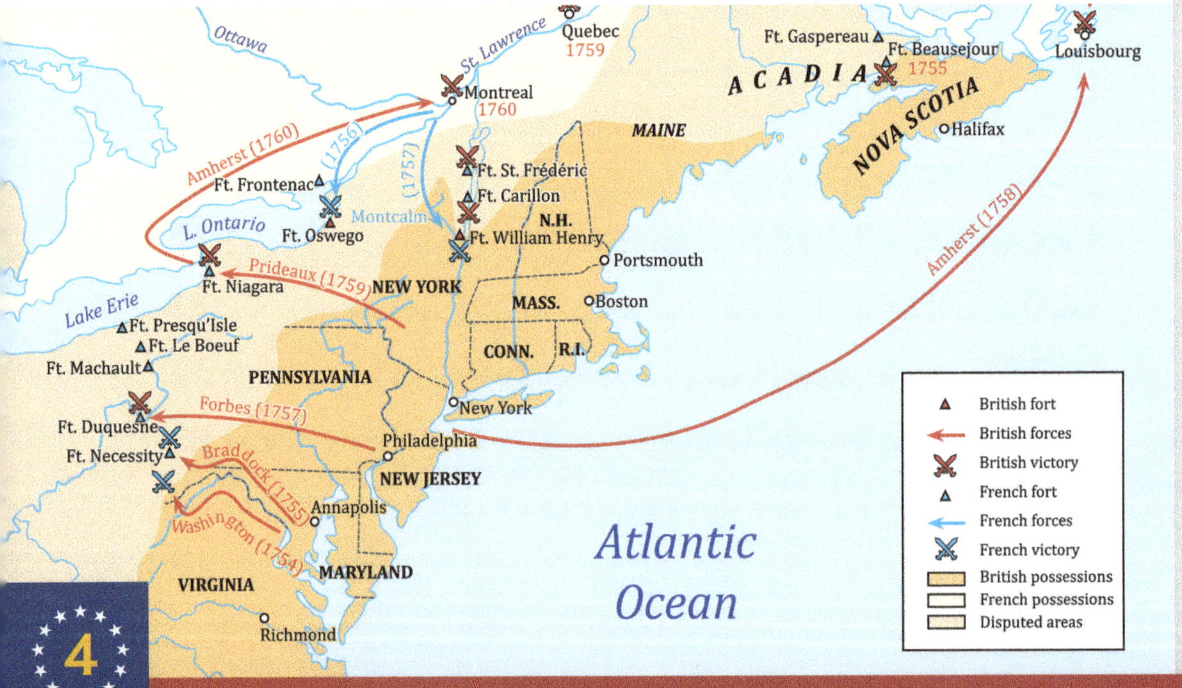

George Washington earned recognition for his service in the French and Indian War. In this painting, he's shown on horseback during the battle of Monongahela in 1755.

Stamp Act of 1765, the British Parliament, or governing body, began to impose taxes on the colonies to raise money to repay this debt. The colonists resisted the new taxes, believing "taxation without representation" in British Parliament was unfair.

To punish the colonies for their resistance, the British imposed new laws that became known as the Intolerable Acts. They closed the harbor in Boston, Massachusetts, required colonists to house British soldiers, and **expanded** British control in other ways.

In 1774, representatives from every colony except Georgia came together to form the First Continental Congress. These **delegates** discussed problems facing the colonies and how to demand fair treatment from King George III.

CHAPTER TWO

GEORGIA'S PLACE IN THE STRUGGLE

No delegates from Georgia were at the First Continental Congress. Georgia was the newest of the 13 colonies and many Georgians were loyal to Britain and grateful for British protection against Native Americans. But the more resistance in the other colonies grew, the more concerned Georgians became.

In 1770, British officers shot at Boston colonials **rallying** against British taxes, killing five of them. This event is called the Boston Massacre. In 1773, colonials destroyed 342 chests of British tea in what became known as the Boston Tea Party. The Boston Port Act, one of the Intolerable Acts, was designed to punish rebels for the Boston Tea Party. The act closed Boston's harbor until the British were repaid for the lost tea.

After the Intolerable Acts were passed, Georgians stood with the residents of Boston and sent wagonloads of food and clothing from Savannah to Boston from 1774 to 1775.

This painting shows the Boston Tea Party, which took place on December 16, 1773. Colonial rebels in Boston disguised themselves as American Indians, snuck onto English trade ships, and destroyed their cargo.

CHAPTER THREE

THE WAR BEGINS

The Revolutionary War began with the Battles of Lexington and Concord, which were fought on April 19, 1775. Soon afterward, the Second Continental Congress met and created the Continental army, which would be led by General George Washington. The Battle of Bunker Hill, which was fought between the New England **militia** and British soldiers, was the first major battle of the war. Although the battle was won by the British, it inspired many Georgia colonists to join the fight.

On May 11, 1775, a group of 30 rebels met in Savannah, Georgia, to discuss their plans to join the revolution. They called themselves the Sons of Liberty, a name also used by other rebel groups in various colonies. They broke into the city's stores of gunpowder and shared it with revolutionaries from South Carolina. Georgia colonists were armed and ready to battle the British.

This drawing shows Savannah as it appeared during the early years of the Georgia colony in the 1700s. By the time the Revolutionary War began, Savannah was one of the most important ports in the Southern Colonies.

CHAPTER FOUR

THE BATTLE OF THE RICE BOATS

In January 1776, British warships entered the Savannah River. Savannah governor James Wright was a Loyalist, or a colonist who sided with Britain. Fearing British **invasion**, the colonists arrested Wright. Colonel Lachlan McIntosh was chosen to plan the city's defense against British attack.

Instead of invading the city, on March 2, 1776, the British took over trade ships in Savannah harbor. Because the ships were carrying rice, this came to be called the Battle of the Rice Boats. As part of the revolution, Americans had cut off trade with Britain, so the British were trying to steal the rice. The Americans tried to burn and destroy the ships before the goods could be stolen, but several were lost. The British took the ships and their cargo to supply troops. Governor Wright escaped Savannah on one of the British ships, leaving Georgia free of British control—at least for the time being.

James Wright was the last royal governor of Georgia.

CHAPTER FIVE

THE FOUNDING DOCUMENTS

On July 4,1776, the Second Continental Congress approved the Declaration of Independence. This document announced that the colonies were now independent.

The three Georgians present at the Second Continental Congress were Button Gwinnett, George Walton, and Lyman Hall. Button Gwinnett was an English-born colonist who was appointed commander of Georgia's militia in 1776. George Walton, a lawyer, served as secretary of the Georgia **Provincial** Congress. Lyman Hall was a respected doctor who helped organize medical resources for the Continental army. Walton, Gwinnett, and Hall signed the Declaration of Independence as Georgia representatives.

The Second Continental Congress also drafted the Articles of Confederation, which would serve as the first constitution of the United States until the U.S. Constitution was ratified in 1788.

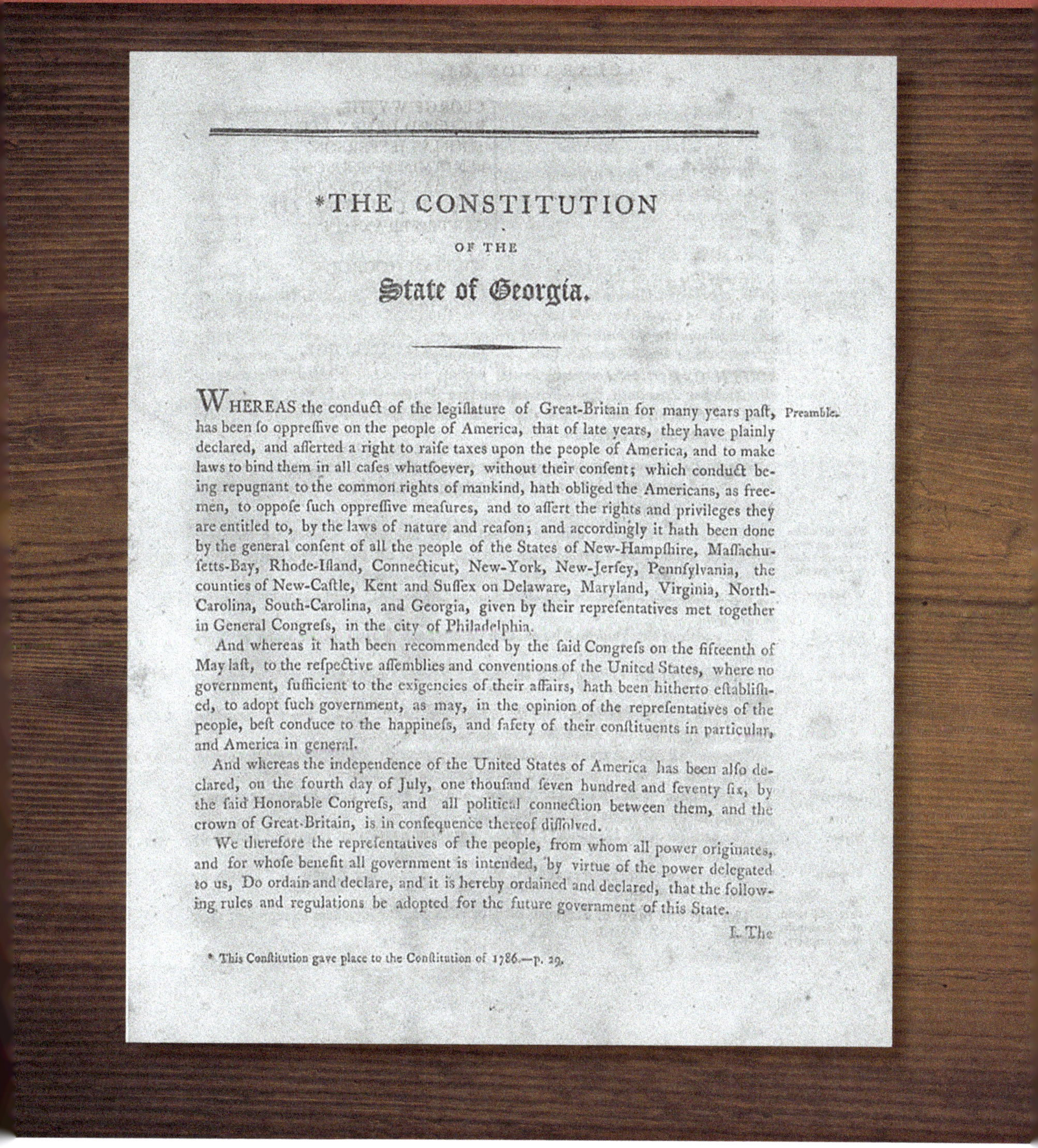

*THE CONSTITUTION

OF THE

State of Georgia.

WHEREAS the conduct of the legiſlature of Great-Britain for many years paſt, has been ſo oppreſſive on the people of America, that of late years, they have plainly declared, and aſſerted a right to raiſe taxes upon the people of America, and to make laws to bind them in all caſes whatſoever, without their conſent; which conduct being repugnant to the common rights of mankind, hath obliged the Americans, as freemen, to oppoſe ſuch oppreſſive meaſures, and to aſſert the rights and privileges they are entitled to, by the laws of nature and reaſon; and accordingly it hath been done by the general conſent of all the people of the States of New-Hampſhire, Maſſachuſetts-Bay, Rhode-Iſland, Connecticut, New-York, New-Jerſey, Pennſylvania, the counties of New-Caſtle, Kent and Suſſex on Delaware, Maryland, Virginia, North-Carolina, South-Carolina, and Georgia, given by their repreſentatives met together in General Congreſs, in the city of Philadelphia. Preamble.

And whereas it hath been recommended by the ſaid Congreſs on the fifteenth of May laſt, to the reſpective aſſemblies and conventions of the United States, where no government, ſufficient to the exigencies of their affairs, hath been hitherto eſtabliſhed, to adopt ſuch government, as may, in the opinion of the repreſentatives of the people, beſt conduce to the happineſs, and ſafety of their conſtituents in particular, and America in general.

And whereas the independence of the United States of America has been alſo declared, on the fourth day of July, one thouſand ſeven hundred and ſeventy ſix, by the ſaid Honorable Congreſs, and all political connection between them, and the crown of Great-Britain, is in conſequence thereof diſſolved.

We therefore the repreſentatives of the people, from whom all power originates, and for whoſe benefit all government is intended, by virtue of the power delegated to us, Do ordain and declare, and it is hereby ordained and declared, that the following rules and regulations be adopted for the future government of this State.

I. The

* This Conſtitution gave place to the Conſtitution of 1786.—p. 29.

Seven months after the declaration was signed, Georgian delegates adopted their own state constitution. It was rewritten several times over the years.

CHAPTER SIX

AMERICA'S ALLIES

In 1777, American forces had a few notable victories. In October 1777, a British army **surrendered** to the Americans at Saratoga, New York. As a result of this and other victories, France entered the war in February 1778 as an ally of the Americans.

The French weren't the only foreign soldiers to join the revolutionary cause. Count Casimir Pulaski was an important Polish commander who left Europe to join the Continental army. Born in Poland in 1745, Pulaski volunteered to help the Americans in 1777. He became the leader of the cavalry, or the part of an army made up of soldiers trained to fight on horseback, in George Washington's army. Before this time, American soldiers didn't have an official cavalry. Pulaski's service helped lead to its establishment in the United States. Pulaski was wounded at the **siege** of Savannah, Georgia, and died a few days later.

Pulaski was inspired to fight alongside the Americans after meeting Benjamin Franklin in Paris, France. Franklin recommended Pulaski to Washington. After Pulaski proved his skills in battle, Congress made him a brigadier general.

CHAPTER SEVEN

NEW BRITISH STRATEGY

British commanders were very concerned about France entering the war. They knew that the **alliance** with France would tip the odds in the Americans' favor. They decided to change their **strategy**. Until the summer of 1778, they had fought mostly in the northern and middle states, believing it important to crush the large numbers of American fighters there. After the failure at Saratoga, they decided to go on the offensive in the American South. The British believed there were more Loyalists in the southern states than in the northern ones.

In the autumn of 1778, the British sent forces north from Florida, which they had acquired from Spain in 1763. The first British attempt to invade Georgia failed, but the second, in December 1778, was a major success. The British captured the important city of Savannah. They were helped by a slave named Quamino Dolly.

This illustration shows an African American soldier and a British soldier during the American Revolutionary War. Some African American slaves joined the British army because they were promised freedom. Others fought for American forces.

CHAPTER EIGHT

THE BATTLE OF KETTLE CREEK

The Battle of Kettle Creek took place on February 14, 1779, in Wilkes County, Georgia. On that morning, about 600 Loyalists were camped at Kettle Creek. They were on their way to join the British forces in Augusta, Georgia, which was under British control at the time. The Loyalists were led by James Boyd of South Carolina. Boyd had been paid by the British to find southern Loyalists to join the fight.

Boyd's Loyalists were attacked by a group of militiamen from South Carolina and Georgia. The militiamen were led by Lieutenant Colonel Elijah Clarke, Colonel Andrew Pickens, and Colonel John Dooly. When Boyd was wounded, the Loyalists fled, but 150 were taken prisoner. The Battle of Kettle Creek was an important victory for the Americans. The victory made other southern Loyalists think twice about fighting for the British.

In 1930, the federal government made Kettle Creek a historic site.

CHAPTER NINE

THE SIEGE OF SAVANNAH

The capture of Savannah by British troops under the command of General Augustine Prevost shifted the war's focus from the North to the South. The commanders of the Continental army began to send northern forces to take back the South from British invasion.

The siege of Savannah in autumn 1779, during which American forces tried to take back the city, was the most important revolutionary battle to take place in Georgia. Casimir Pulaski, Arthur Dillon (who commanded a regiment of Irish troops fighting for France), and French allies fought alongside the Americans. To aid them, a fleet of French ships under the command of French Admiral Charles d'Estaing approached the Georgia coast. The French and American allied troops launched a series of attacks but were unable to retake Savannah. The British kept control of the city, which allowed them to expand farther South.

The siege of Savannah raged from September 16 to October 18, 1779.

CHAPTER TEN

HIGH TIDE FOR THE BRITISH

The British commanders were pleased with the success of their strategy in the South. British troops attacked Charleston, South Carolina, in the spring of 1780. When the city fell in May, roughly 5,000 American troops laid down their weapons. It was the largest American surrender of the war. The British commanders' hold on Charleston allowed them to rally American Loyalists in the area.

The British quickly fanned out into the countryside, winning one **skirmish** after another. Their biggest success came at the Battle of Camden, South Carolina, in August 1780. Led by Major General Charles Cornwallis, the British completely crushed an American force led by Major General Horatio Gates. While holding Camden, the British were able to collect supplies and weapons. At that point, it seemed as though the British couldn't lose. Their hold on the South was a threat to Georgian rebels.

Cornwallis was a veteran of the Seven Years' War. Although he didn't agree with British taxation policies, he served in the British army and worked to end the revolution.

CHAPTER ELEVEN

THE SIEGE OF AUGUSTA

By the end of 1780, half of Georgia was back under British control. British and Loyalist forces held the city of Augusta, Georgia, where they built Fort Cornwallis to defend it against American forces.

Beginning in April, the patriot militia set up camp outside Augusta under the command of Colonel Micajah

ANDREW PICKENS

HENRY LEE

Williamson, who was later joined by General Elijah Clarke. Meanwhile, General Andrew Pickens blocked off the city from British support sent from South Carolina. In May of 1781, Lieutenant Colonel Henry "Light-Horse Harry" Lee joined forces with Pickens. Together they attacked nearby Fort Galphin and Fort Grierson. Clarke, Lee, and Pickens had a 30-foot tower built from which they could attack Fort Cornwallis. On June 1, 1781, the patriots began firing down on Fort Cornwallis from high in their tower. The Americans captured Fort Cornwallis on June 5, winning control of Augusta, Georgia.

CHAPTER TWELVE

THE TALE OF NANCY HART

From a backcountry cabin, a story of patriot victory inspired Georgians to continue the fight for independence. Nancy Hart was the wife of Benjamin Hart, who was a soldier serving under General Clarke. She was in her frontier home when she saw Loyalists approaching. According to legend, the Loyalists demanded entry to the cabin and forced Hart to serve them food and wine. As she did, Hart passed their muskets out the window to her daughter. When they realized what she was doing, one of the men tried to attack her. Hart shot two Loyalists and held the others at bay while her daughter ran for help. The remaining Loyalists were put to death soon after.

It's unclear how much of this story is based on fact. Nancy Hart became a character of folklore, with many patriotic deeds credited to her.

Named after Nancy Hart, Hart County, Georgia, is the only county in Georgia that's named for a woman.

CHAPTER THIRTEEN

CORNWALLIS'S SURRENDER

In the summer of 1781, General Cornwallis took his forces north to Yorktown, Virginia. In Yorktown, Cornwallis and his army were surrounded by a French-American force and a French war fleet commanded by Admiral Francois-Joseph-Paul de Grasse. The battle ended in American victory. The French-American alliance was successful, and General Cornwallis surrendered his entire army on October 19, 1781. Yorktown was the last major battle of the American Revolution. Soon after this loss, the British began to draw back and start peace agreements.

The British were beaten, but they held sections of Georgia right to the bitter end. The British left Savannah, Georgia, on July 11, 1782. The Treaty of Paris was signed in 1783, officially ending the war. A large number of Loyalists from each city accompanied the British as they left. In the case of Savannah, the fleeing Loyalists numbered more than 6,000.

This painting, which was made in 1820, shows the British surrendering after the Battle of Yorktown. General George Washington is shown on horseback beside the American flag.

CHAPTER FOURTEEN

GEORGIA AT WAR'S END

Georgia had not been the most enthusiastic of the 13 colonies at the start of the war, but the state paid a high price for its participation. Several thousand Georgians had been killed and many farms had been destroyed by British and Loyalist forces or by Americans who wished to prevent them from falling into British hands. The new state was a long way from being stable.

Many American patriots had come south to fight under the various Continental army generals. Quite a few of these veterans decided to remain in Georgia. They applied for, and usually received, large grants of land for their war service. As a result, the white population of Georgia increased in the years immediately following the Revolutionary War. What would this mean for Georgians in the years of nation building to come?

GLOSSARY

alliance (uh-LY-unts) A group of countries working together for a common goal.

debt (DEHT) Something owed.

delegate (DEH-lih-get) A person sent to a meeting or convention to represent others.

expand (ihk-SPAND) To become bigger.

imperial (im-PEER-ee-ul) Having to do with an emperor or empire.

invasion (in-VAY-zhun) The entry of an armed force into an area in order to take control of it.

militia (muh-LIH-shuh) A group of volunteers or citizen soldiers who are trained and ready to fight in emergencies.

provincial (pruh-VIN-shul) Belonging to a certain part of the country.

rally (RA-lee) To rouse support for a common purpose.

revolution (reh-vuh-LOO-shun) A movement to overthrow an established government.

siege (SEEJ) The operations of an army around a place for the purpose of forcing its occupants to give up.

skirmish (SKUR-mish) A brief fight.

strategy (STRA-tuh-jee) A plan of action to achieve a goal.

surrender (suh-REN-der) To give up.

INDEX

PRIMARY SOURCE LIST

Page 11
James Wright (1716–1785). Andrea Soldi. Oil on canvas. Now kept at Telfair Museums, Savannah, Georgia.

Page 13
The Constitution of the State of Georgia. Watkins, Robert and George Watkins. *A Digest of the Laws of the State of Georgia*. Philadelphia: Printed by R. Aitkin, No. 22, Market Street, 1800.

Page 15
Count Pulaski. White, Rev. George. Historical Collections of Georgia. New York, NY: Pudney & Russell Publishers, 1855.

WEBSITES

Due to the changing nature of Internet links, PowerKids Press has developed an online list of websites related to the subject of this book. This site is updated regularly. Please use this link to access the list: www.powerkidslinks.com/sog/amrev